# Dog Treats

## The BARKtender's Guide® to Easy Homemade Pupcakes

Boo zeHound and Elizabeth Dodwell

Boo zeHound and Elizabeth Dodwell

# TABLE OF CONTENTS

# PUBLISHERS NOTES

The BARKtender's Guide®

FIRST PUBLISHED BY SPEEDY PUBLISHING LLC © 2013
ISBN-9781630227210

For corrections, book orders, bulk discounts, author appearances, inquiries or interviews, contact publisher by email or regular mail at:
**Speedy Publishing, LLC,** 40 E. Main St., #1156, Newark, DE 19711
www.speedypublishing.co
Manufactured in the United States.

**www.BARKtendersGuide.com**
**www.facebook.com/TheBARKtendersGuide**
twitter: @The_BARKtender

Photos by Scott Bedenbaugh of Pix2Go Studios, Pix2Go.com and stock photos

# DEDICATION

To my own two little pupcakes, Vinny and Coco

# CHAPTER 1- GRRREETINGS!

Angel, Vinny and Coco, with whom my husband and I share our lives, all came to us from Southern Hope Humane Society in Georgia (southernhopehumane.com). Earning the trio's trust and love has been a truly humbling journey and we are constantly amazed at our canines' capacity for forgiveness.

Food has been an integral part in our pups' transformation. Let's face it, it's one of the most fundamental ways in which we connect with our dogs. Not only do we provide them with daily sustenance, but we offer food to assist in training, as a reward for good behavior and because it helps reinforce the special bond between us.

Researching and testing the BARKtender recipes has been a definite family affair. Somehow, as soon as I start gathering ingredients for pupcakes, the dogs know and line up in the kitchen keeping a careful eye on the proceedings. The moment the oven door is opened to remove the baked treats they are a bundle of barely suppressed excitement.

These recipes have all been developed with your pooch's health in mind. You'll find a number of recipes use gluten-free flour; dairy products are low fat; fresh and organic ingredients replace over-processed products. However, it should be stressed that these *are* treats, *not* a substitute for your dog's daily diet.

Much gratitude is owed to several people without whose help *The BARKtender's Guide*® would never have made it to publication. Photographer, Scott Bedenbaugh of Pix2Go.com, for the endless hours he patiently spent ensuring the pupcakes look brilliant in print. Also, for debugging my computer and saving it from the scrap heap, along with my sanity. Suzanne Stevens who owns and operates Sweets on the Square in Lawrenceville, GA, for decorating the pupcakes in The BARKtender's Guide® with some amazing original designs and other popular designs. She also makes some of the best cupcakes you've ever tasted. Dr Nancy Churchill of Gwinnett Animal Hospital in

Boo zeHound and Elizabeth Dodwell Snellville, GA for advice on foods that are safe for dogs and for helping keep my "kids" safe and well all these years. Robin Taylor, owner of Gwinnett Pet Watchers, Lawrenceville, GA for her invaluable friendship, encouragement and eternal optimism and for allowing her dogs to be part of the Doggie Tasting Team that approved these recipes. And most of all, my husband, Alex Markovich, who makes all things possible.

Elizabeth Dodwell
Author, Speaker, Humorist, Dog maniac

# CHAPTER 2- THE BARE BONES

**Note:** Those of you familiar with the BARKtender's Guide®
to Homemade Dogtails and Muttinis will know the following
recipes. As they are essential to a number of our Pupcake
recipes, we've also included them here.

Broth is a staple for a number of recipes in *The
BARKtender's Guide®*. It's really nutritious, easy to make
and batches of broth can be divided into small amounts and
frozen for future use. Boo uses small freezer baggies that he
first labels and dates and from which he removes the air
before sealing. This is a great way to pack a lot of broth into
a small space. (*Hint:* don't place baggies directly on wire
racks in the freezer or they'll get stuck. Put them on a flat
surface).

Yes, you can find organic stock in the store. However,
it will contain onion, salt, pepper and other ingredients that
are *ah-ahs* for your pet. Instead, get friendly with your
butcher and fishmonger and ask for meaty bones and fish
parts that might otherwise be thrown away. So what if you
pay a little? Rover will kiss you all over for being such a
wonderful pawrent.

# Basic Meat Broth

This is a basic recipe for any meat broth.

***What you need:***

- 3 - 4 lbs of meaty bones
- Cold water

***What to do:***

- In a large heavy pan cover the bones with cold water by about 2 inches
- Bring to a simmer (not a boil) over medium heat, skimming off the scum that rises to the top
- Partially cover the pot and continue to slow simmer for 2 - 3 hours
- Check occasionally and skim if necessary. If the water level drops below the bones add a little more *hot* water
- When done, strain the broth to remove the meat and bones
- **Be sure to discard the bones\*** though it's OK to save the meat to give to Bowser
- Refrigerate the broth overnight. The fat will rise to the top and solidify
- Remove and discard the fat, the broth should now be gel-like.
- At this stage, you can divide the broth into containers and refrigerate or freeze 'til needed. Or, if you want to remove any traces of remaining fat, bring the broth to room temperature and strain through a coffee filter 'til completely clear, then refrigerate or freeze

\*NEVER give your dog cooked bones. They can easily splinter and cause very serious injuries.

# Basic Fish Broth

***What you need:***

- About 3 lbs of any combination of fish spines, heads and tails (do **not** use shellfish)
- 1 gallon cold water

***What to do:***

- Wash tails and heads in cold water and cut out any gills (they tend to be bitter)
- In a large pot add all the fish pieces with the water
- Bring to a boil, cover and simmer on low for one hour
- If the water level drops too low, add a little *hot* water
- When done, strain through a fine mesh strainer lined with cheesecloth or a large coffee filter; discard the bones, skin, etc.
- Refrigerate or freeze the broth as needed

# Basic Vegetable Broth

***What you need:***

- Any combination of "safe" vegetables (see below) but definitely NO **onion**
- Cold water

*What to do*:

- Wash the vegetables and chop them roughly (no need to peel anything but cut out any bad parts)
- Put them in a heavy pot and cover with water by about two inches
- Bring to a slow simmer, cover and leave for about 1 hour, stirring occasionally
- Strain through a fine sieve with cheesecloth or a coffee filter
- Refrigerate or freeze the broth as needed

**Safe vegetables include:**

Asparagus - beetroot - broccoli - cabbage - carrots - cauliflower - celery - green beans - kale - parsley - squash - sweet potato.

If in any doubt about an ingredient - check with your vet.

No creature is more generous with love than a puppy

## Just a note:

Our doggie pupcake recipes have been created with an average to large size dog in mind. This means you will need to adjust portions for your Toy Yorkie or St Bernard.

**Always keep in mind** that any time you give your BFF a food that he or she has not had before (or make any change in diet, for that matter) begin with just a small amount and introduce the food gradually. It's a myth that dogs have cast iron stomachs (OK, maybe yours does) and changes in diet can sometimes cause digestive problems.

# CHAPTER 3- MEATY PUPCAKES

## "Where's the beef?"

Although our Pupcake recipes have been divided into Meaty, Cheesy, Fishy, Nutty and Fruity, you'll find a number of them will fit into more than one category. Keep in mind, also, that it's OK to substitute gluten-free flours for wheat flour or vice versa depending on your dog's needs or preferences.

Boo zeHound and Elizabeth Dodwell

# Give a Dog a Bone

## *What you need:*

- 1 3/4 cups gluten-free, multi-purpose flour
- 1 tsp baking soda
- 1 tsp baking powder
- 1 cup low-fat cottage cheese
- 2 jars (2.5 oz size) turkey baby food, or you can puree fresh turkey meat with a little water
- 2 eggs
- 2 tbs black molasses (Black Treacle)
- 1 tbsp vegetable oil
- 1 tbsp flax seed oil* Veg oil
- 2 tsp bone meal (food grade) Amazon

## *What to do:*

- preheat oven to 350 F and line a muffin pan with baking cups
- whisk together all the dry ingredients
- create a well in the center of the flour mix and add all other ingredients
- combine everything with the whisk or wooden spoon 'til well blended
- spoon the batter into the cups to about 3/4 full
- bake for 18- 20 minutes or until a toothpick inserted in a pupcake comes out clean
- cool in the pan for a few minutes, then move to a cooling rack
- before serving push a chew treat in the middle; we like Merrick Flossies
- *OK to use just veg oil

Yields 12 - 15 pupcakes, or about 25 minis

# Sit! Stay! Eat!

## "We'll go arf and arf. I'll take the top arf, you get the bottom. Fair enough?"

### *What you need:*

- 1 cup gluten free flour
- 1tsp baking soda
- 1 tsp baking powder
- 2 jars (2.5 oz each) chicken baby food
- ¼ - ½ cup chicken broth (recipe in Chapter 2)
- ¼ cup vegetable oil
- 2 tbsp molasses
- ¾ cup mashed sweet potato
- 1 level tsp spirulina powder

### *What to do:*

- Preheat the oven to 350 F
- Prepare a mini muffin pan with baking cups

- Whisk all the dry ingredients together in a large bowl
- Add the chicken, chicken broth, molasses and oil and blend in to the flour mix
- Stir in the sweet potato then beat the mix with a wooden spoon 'til the batter is smooth
- Fill the baking cups and bake for 10 - 12 minutes or until a toothpick comes out clean from the middle of a pupcake
- Cool for 3 or 4 minutes in the pan then move to a cooling rack

# Pound Pupcakes

*What you need:*

- 1 cup gluten-free flour (eg. King Arthur or Bob's Red Mill)
- ½ tsp baking powder
- ½ tsp baking soda
- ½ cup carrots and peas pureed with a ¼ cup water (or use baby food)
- 1 jar (2.5 oz) baby food chicken, or fresh chicken pureed with a little water
- 1 tsp organic tomato paste
- 1 tbsp dried parsley flakes or 2 tbsp chopped fresh parsley
- 1 raw egg
- 1 cooked egg, chopped small
- 1 cooked egg, sliced

*What to do:*

- preheat the oven to 350 F
- add baking cups to a muffin pan

- whisk the flour, baking powder and baking soda together in a large bowl
- make a "well" in the middle of the dry mix and add all the other ingredients except the chopped egg
- blend the wet and dry ingredients together with a wooden spoon
- when thoroughly mixed, stir in the cooked chopped egg
- drop the mix into standard baking cups
- bake for 15 - 18 minutes, 'til a toothpick comes out clean from the center of a pupcake
- cool in the pan for 2 or 3 minutes then move the pupcakes to a wire rack
- instead of frosting, place a slice of cooked egg on top of each pupcake and add a tiny sprig of parsley

Yields 6 pupcakes

# Macho Mutt

## Real dogs eat Pupcakes...
## and they like little puppies

Boo zeHound and Elizabeth Dodwell
**What you need:**

- 1 cup oat flour*
- ½ cup brown rice flour*
- ½ cup oats
- 1 tsp oat bran
- 2 tsp baking powder
- ½ tsp baking soda
- 4 oz beef liver
- ½ cup pork broth
- ¼ cup vegetable oil
- 2 eggs
- 1 tbsp molasses
- ½ cup mashed potato

**What to do:**

- Preheat the oven to 350 F
- Prepare a muffin pan by lining with baking cups
- Roughly chop the liver and puree with the pork broth then set aside
- Put all the dry ingredients in a large bowl and whisk them together thoroughly
- In a separate bowl mix all the other ingredients
- A little at a time mix the dry ingredients into the wet, adding a little water if needed, so you have a stiff batter
- Fill the baking cups with the batter and bake for 20 - 22 minutes or until a toothpick inserted in the middle of a pupcake comes out clean
- After 2 or 3 minutes move the pupcakes to a wire rack to cool

Yields about 1 dozen pupcakes

*Oat and rice flour are often gluten-free but, if you need to be sure it is safe for your sensitive pup, the packaging should read "Certified gluten-free."

# The Nose Knows

*What you need:*

- 2 ½ cups gluten-free flour
- 1 tsp baking powder
- 1 tsp baking soda
- 1 cup beef broth (see recipe in Chapter 2)
- 1 jar (2.5 oz) beef baby food (or chicken or turkey)
- ¼ cup black molasses
- ¼ cup vegetable oil
- 2 eggs

*What to do:*

- Preheat your oven to 350 F
- Line a muffin pan with baking cups
- In a large bowl, mix the flour, baking powder and baking soda with a whisk
- Make a well in the middle of the dry ingredients and add the broth, baby food, molasses, oil and eggs
- Use the whisk to mix everything together, gradually incorporating the dry ingredients into the batter
- Drop the batter into the baking cups
- Bake for 20 - 25 minutes or until a toothpick comes out clean from the middle of a pupcake
- Let the pupcakes sit in the pan for 3 or 4 minutes before moving to a wire rack to cool

Yields 12 - 14 standard pupcakes

# Three Dog Pupcake

### *What you need:*

- 8 oz ground turkey
- 1 cup Eden Foods canned Organic Black Beans (no salt, low fat), rinsed and drained
- 1 cup mixed lightly steamed vegetables
- 1 cup cooked organic brown rice
- ½ - 1 cup turkey or chicken broth (recipe in Chapter 2)
- 1 egg
- 1½ cups gluten-free flour (try King Arthur or Bob's Red Mill)
- ½ cup rolled oats
- 1 tsp baking powder
- ½ tsp baking soda
- 2 tsp bone meal powder

### *What to do:*

- Preheat the oven to 350 F and prepare muffin pans by lining with baking cups

- Puree the beans and vegetables with ½ cup of broth in a blender
- Add the puree mix to a large bowl with the turkey, rice and egg and mix together well
- In a separate bowl, whisk together the flour, oats, baking powder, baking soda and bone meal powder
- Combine the dry ingredients with the turkey mixture a little at a time. The batter will be quite stiff, so use your hands to knead it and add more broth if the batter seems too dry
- Fill the baking cups
- Bake for 35 - 40 minutes
- Test for doneness by inserting a toothpick in the center of a pupcake. It should come out clean
- Leave the pupcakes in the pan for 2 or 3 minutes before removing to a wire rack to cool

*These really need no frosting but if Buddy must have something, we suggest the cream cheese frosting recipe in Chapter 7. The decoration shown is from the book, 'Hello Cupcake.'*

Yields about 18 pupcakes

# Gone to the Dogs

### *What you need:*

- 1 cup rice flour
- ½ cup oat flour
- 1 tsp baking powder
- ½ tsp baking soda
- 1 jar (2.5 oz) baby food beef or chicken
- ¼ - ½ cup beef or chicken broth (recipe on page 12)
- 1 egg
- 1 cup shredded mixed vegetables*

- 1 tbsp molasses
- 1 tbsp dried parsley or 2 tbsp chopped fresh parsley (or sprinkle of spirulina powder

### *What to do:*

- Preheat oven to 350 F and line a muffin pan with baking cups
- Whisk together all the dry ingredients
- Make a well in the middle of the dry ingredients and add the egg, baby food, ¼ cup of meat broth and molasses
- Beat the wet ingredients together, gradually incorporating the dry mix. If need be, add the additional ¼ cup of meat broth
- Stir in the shredded vegetables and parsley
- Fill your baking cups and bake for 18 - 22 minutes, 'til a toothpick comes out clean from the middle of a pupcake
- Let stand in the muffin pan for a few minutes before removing the pupcakes to a cooling rack

*Safe vegetables for your dog include carrot, peas, squash, green beans, asparagus, broccoli, celery, sprouts

Yields 8 - 10 pupcakes

# CHAPTER 4- CHEESY PUPCAKES

Say Cheese!

Boo zeHound and Elizabeth Dodwell
# Red Rover Pupcakes

### *What you need:*

- 1 ½ cups gluten-free flour
- ½ cup rolled oats
- 2 tsp baking powder
- ½ tsp baking soda
- ½ cup pureed 100% pure pumpkin
- ¼ cup unsweetened, pure beetroot juice (eg. Smart Basics, Dynamic Health and Biotta)
- ¼ cup vegetable oil
- 2 tbsp rice syrup
- 2 eggs
- 1 small cooked sweet potato, chopped, skin on
- 1 cup grated cheddar cheese
- Water, if necessary

### *What to do:*

- Preheat the oven to 400 F
- Line muffin pans with baking cups
- Whisk together the dry ingredients in a large bowl
- Make a well in the center and add the pumpkin, beet juice, oil, syrup and eggs
- Combine wet and dry ingredients so they're well blended
- If the mix is a little dry, add in a tablespoon or two of water
- Stir in the sweet potato and cheese
- Fill the baking cups with the mixture
- Bake for about 15 minutes (10 minutes for mini pupcakes) or 'til a toothpick inserted in a pupcake comes out clean
- Cool for a few minutes in the pan then move to a cooling rack
- Let cool before frosting

Yields about 15 regular pupcakes or 30 minis

*Try these with cream cheese frosting (see Chapter 7) colored with a little carob powder.*

# Woof it Down

### *What you need:*

- 1 ½ cups whole wheat flour
- ¼ cup oatmeal
- 2 tsps baking powder
- ½ tsp baking soda
- 1 lg apple
- ½ cup water
- ½ cup plain low fat yogurt
- ¼ cup vegetable oil

- 2 eggs
- 2 tbsp rice syrup or honey
- 1 cup grated cheddar

### *What to do:*

- Preheat oven to 400 F and line muffin tins with baking cups
- Core and dice the apple and puree with the water then set aside
- In a bowl, whisk together the dry ingredients (flour, oatmeal, baking powder, baking soda)
- Make a well in the flour mix and add the yogurt, oil, honey, eggs and apple puree
- With the whisk, blend wet and dry ingredients together
- When thoroughly blended, add the cheese and mix with a spoon
- Fill the baking cups about ¾ full with the mixture
- Bake for about 20 minutes or until a toothpick inserted in the center of a pupcake comes out clean
- Let the muffins rest for a while, then remove from the pan and cool on a wire rack
- Finish with peanut butter frosting (recipe in Chapter 7)

*Note: Always remember to remove the paper baking cup before giving Bella her treat*

Yields 16 - 18 standard size pupcakes

# Tres Licks Pupcakes

## "I have so got these licked"

### *What you need:*

- 1 cup whole wheat flour
- 1 tsp baking powder
- ¼ tsp baking soda
- ¼ cup plain low-fat yogurt
- 2 ½ tbsp vegetable oil
- 2 tbsp molasses
- 1 lg egg
- ¼ cup fine chopped apple
- ¼ cup grated carrot
- ½ cup grated cheddar cheese

**What to do:**

- Preheat the oven to 350 F and prep a muffin pan by lining it with baking cups
- In a large bowl, stir together the dry ingredients
- Add the yogurt, oil, molasses and egg
- Blend all the ingredients together thoroughly
- Gradually stir in the apple, carrot and cheese
- Drop the mixture into the baking cups
- Bake for 15 minutes then remove and quickly sprinkle a little grated cheddar on top of each pupcake
- Return to the oven for another 5 minutes or until a toothpick inserted in the middle of a pupcake comes out clean
- Let sit for 2 or 3 minutes then move to a cooling rack

Yields 10 pupcakes

# You Can't Lick It

**What you need:**

- ½ cup oat flour (look for "Certified gluten free" on the package)
- ½ cup tapioca flour
- 1 tsp baking powder
- 1 tsp baking soda
- ½ cup cheddar cheese
- 1 jar (2.5 oz) beef baby food
- 2 tbsp vegetable oil
- 1 egg
- ½ cup shredded carrots

### *What to do:*

- Preheat oven to 350 F
- Line a muffin pan with baking cups
- Whisk together the dry ingredients
- Make a well in the center of the flour mix and drop in the beef, oil and egg
- Gradually blend the ingredients together
- Mix in the carrots and cheese
- Fill the baking cups and bake for 20 minutes or 'til a toothpick inserted into a pupcake pulls out clean
- When done, let sit for a few minutes before removing to a cooling rack

Yields about 20 pupcakes

"No, Frank. There's nothing stuck in your teeth"

# CHAPTER 5- FISHY PUPCAKES

## "What does a guy have to do to get a fishy pupcake around here?"

Boo zeHound and Elizabeth Dodwell

# Bowser Wowser

### *What you need:*

- 1 ½ cups gluten free flour
- 1 tsp baking soda
- 1 tsp baking powder
- ¼ cup flaked tuna (fresh cooked or 'no salt added' canned tuna)
- ¼ cup vegetable oil
- ½ cup low fat cottage cheese
- 1 egg
- ½ cup fresh or frozen peas

### *What to do:*

- Preheat the oven to 350 F and prepare muffin pans by lining with baking cups
- Add the flour, baking powder and baking soda to a large bowl and whisk to mix
- Make a well in the center of the dry mix and drop in the oil, egg and cottage cheese
- Whisk together and gradually incorporate the dry ingredients into the wet mix
- Stir in the tuna and peas
- Drop the batter into the baking cups to ¾ full
- Bake for 20 -25 minutes, 'til a toothpick inserted into a pupcake comes out clean
- Cool in the pan for 2 or 3 minutes, then move to a wire rack

Yields 10 pupcakes

# Well Tickle My Tummy

## "Ready when you are!"

### *What you need:*

- 1 cup oat flour
- ¾ cup tapioca flour
- ½ cup rolled oats
- 2 tsp baking powder
- ½ tsp baking soda
- ½ cup cooked, flaked salmon*
- 1 - 2 tbsp of the salmon water
- ¼ cup vegetable oil
- 2 eggs
- 1 cup grated cheddar cheese
- ½ cup chopped, cooked green beans

### *What to do:*

- Preheat the oven to 375 F and line muffin pans with baking cups
- In a large bowl, whisk all the dry ingredients together

- Make a well in the center of the bowl and drop in the eggs, oil and 1 tbsp of salmon water
- Mix well and gradually incorporate the flour into the batter, adding a little more salmon water if necessary
- When thoroughly combined, stir in the flaked salmon, green beans and ½ cup of the cheese
- Fill the baking cakes about ¾ full with batter
- Bake for 15 minutes, remove and sprinkle the remaining ½ cup of cheese on top
- Return to the oven and bake an additional 5 minutes or until a toothpick inserted in the pupcakes comes out clean

*Steam or microwave in just a little water with no additives. Save the water. Let cool. *Or* you can use canned, no salt added salmon, available at health food stores or online.

Yields about 1 dozen pupcakes

# CHAPTER 6- NUTTY AND FRUITY PUPCAKES

## "Give me pupcakes or the slipper goes!"

# Gourmutt Peanut

## *What you need:*

- ¾ cup oat flour
- ½ cup brown rice flour
- ¼ cup tapioca flour
- 1 tsp cinnamon
- 1 tsp baking powder
- ½ tsp baking soda
- ¼ cup 100% pure peanut butter
- ½ - ¾ cup chicken broth (recipe in Chapter 2)
- 1 egg
- ¼ cup bacon pieces (optional)

***What to do:***

- Preheat the oven to 350 F
- Line muffin pans with baking cups
- Add all the dry ingredients to a large bowl and whisk together well
- In a separate bowl, beat the egg with the peanut butter and ½ cup of chicken broth 'til completely smooth
- Add the peanut butter mix to the dry ingredients and stir together thoroughly. If the mixture is too stiff add in the additional chicken broth
- Stir in the bacon pieces
- Pour the batter into your baking cups
- Bake mini pupcakes for 10 - 12 minutes, standard pupcakes for 18 - 20 minutes, or 'til a toothpick inserted in a pupcake comes out clean
- When done, remove from the oven and let stand for a few minutes in the pan before placing cupcakes on a cooling rack
- Finish with a simple cream cheese frosting (recipe in chapter 7)

Yields 7 or 8 regular size or 15 - 16 mini pupcakes

# Droolin' On a Sunday Afternoon

***What you need:***

- 1 cup whole wheat flour
- 1 tsp baking soda
- ¼ cup 100% pure peanut butter, no sugar or additives
- ¼ cup vegetable oil
- 1 egg

Boo zeHound and Elizabeth Dodwell

- ½ cup pureed carrot (or you can use baby food carrot)
- ½ cup shredded carrot
- 1 tsp non-alcoholic vanilla
- 2 tbsp rice syrup

### *What to do:*

- preheat oven to 350 F and put baking cups in a muffin pan
- whisk together the flour and baking soda
- make a well in the center of the flour mix and add in the remaining ingredients; mix thoroughly
- fill the baking cups about ¾ full
- bake for about 18-20 minutes or until a toothpick inserted into the pupcakes comes out clean
- let sit for 3 or 4 minutes then remove the pupcakes to a cooling rack
- when cool, lightly frost with cottage cheese frosting (recipe in Chapter 7)
- top with a little crumbled bacon

Yields 12 standard pupcakes or about 25 minis

# Pawty Animal Pupcakes

### *What you need:*

- 1 cup gluten-free, all-purpose flour (eg. King Arthur or Bob's Red Mill)
- 1/4 cup rolled oats
- 1 tsp baking powder
- 1/2 tsp baking soda
- 1/2 tsp cinnamon
- 1/4 cup organic plain (unsweetened) low-fat yogurt
- 1/4 cup vegetable oil
- 1 cup chopped **seedless** watermelon (don't drain)
- 1 tsp alcohol-free vanilla (readily available online and at many local health food stores or make your own with the recipe that follows)
- 2 tbsp rice syrup
- 1 egg

### *What to do:*

- Preheat oven to 350 F

- Blend all the dry ingredients in a large bowl with a hand whisk
- Make a well in the flour mix and add the yogurt, oil, vanilla, rice syrup and egg
- Whisk together, gradually incorporating the dry ingredients
- With a spoon or spatula, blend in the watermelon
- If the mix is too moist, add a little more flour
- Spoon into small baking cups
- Bake for 10 - 12 minutes. Pupcakes are done when a toothpick inserted in the middle comes out clean
- Move to a cooling rack
- Frost with a plain cream cheese frosting (recipe in Chapter 7)
- Sprinkle just a tiny bit of cinnamon powder on top

Yields 20 - 25 mini pupcakes

# Vanilla Extract

***What you need:***

- 2 vanilla beans
- 12 oz glycerin
- 4 oz warm water

***What to do:***

- Mix the glycerin and warm water in a glass jar
- Slit beans down the middle to expose the seeds and add to the liquid
- Seal, shake and set in a dark place (or use a dark jar)
- Shake every few days
- Your vanilla extract will be ready in 1 month

# Dog Day Afternoon

### What you need:

- 4 cups dry dog food*
- 1 cup wet dog food*
- 1 cup mashed sweet potato
- 1 cup mashed ripe banana
- 1/3 cup rice syrup
- 1/3 cup canola
- 1 apple, finely chopped

### What to do:

- Pre-heat oven to 350 F
- Thoroughly mix all ingredients except the apple. If the mix seems too dry, add a little water
- Stir in the apple
- Fill baking cups set in muffin tins
- Cook for 15 - 20 minutes or 'til a toothpick inserted in the middle comes out clean
- Let the pupcakes sit for a few minutes, then move to a rack to cool
- No frosting needed. These may not look great to you but Lulu will love them

Yields 10 - 12 pupcakes

*Your pup's favorite, quality brand
*Ground Entrée-style seems to bind the mix better than Gravy-style*

Boo zeHound and Elizabeth Dodwell

# Petit Paws

***What you need:***

- 1 cup whole wheat flour
- 1 tsp baking soda
- 1 heaping tsp carob powder
- ½ cup low fat plain yogurt
- ½ cup 100 % pure pumkpin (NOT pie filling)
- 1 egg
- 2 tbsp vegetable oil
- 2 tbsp molasses
- ½ tsp non-alcoholic vanilla
- Water, if necessary

***What to do:***

- preheat the oven to 350 F
- line a muffin pan with baking cups
- put all the dry ingredients in a large bowl and whisk them together
- create a well in the middle of the dry mix and add the yogurt, egg, oil, molasses, pumpkin and vanilla
- beat the wet ingredients together and gradually incorporate the dry mix into the batter, adding a little water if the batter seems too stiff.
- fill the baking cups and bake for about 20 minutes for standard size or 12 minutes for mini pupcakes. The pupcakes are done when a toothpick inserted into their middle comes out clean
- remove from the oven and let sit in the muffin pan for 3 or 4 minutes then place on a cooling rack

Yields about 24 mini pupcakes and 10 standard size

***To create the 'Lollipup:'***

- Cover a mini pupcake with an even layer of peanut butter and cream cheese frosting

- Center a heart-shaped dog biscuit (we used *Get Naked* chicken flavor) on the top and press into the frosting
- Use a decorating bag to pipe dots of frosting on the biscuit where the eyes, nose and tongue will be
- Cut pieces of dog treats (Pur Luv Mini Bones) to finish the eyes and nose
- The tongue is a candy heart (if you're concerned about sugar in the candy, remove it before giving the lollipup)
- Take another heart-shaped biscuit and break it in half for the earsInsert a rawhide stick or a carrot stick in the pupcake and Princess now has a Lollipup

# Pineapple Upside Down Pupcake

### *What you need:*

- ½ cup brown rice flour
- ½ cup oat flour
- 1 tsp baking soda
- 2 jars (2.5 oz) ham or chicken baby food

- ¼ cup vegetable oil
- 1 tsp vegetable oil for coating the baking cups
- unsweetened pineapple pieces, about 40
- 1 tbsp rice syrup
- 1 egg
- blueberries for garnish

### What to do:

- Preheat oven to 350 F
- Add a very light coating of oil to the inside of *foil* baking cups then place them in a muffin pan
- In a large bowl whisk together the flour and baking soda
- Blend in the baby food, vegetable oil, syrup and egg
- Lay three pineapple pieces on the bottom of each baking cup
- Spoon the batter into the baking cups and create a slight indentation in the top. You want the pupcakes to be fairly flat when cooked as the top will become the bottom
- Bake for about 20 minutes or until a toothpick inserted in the middle of a pupcake comes out clean
- Let sit for 2 or 3 minutes then move to a cooling rack
- When cool, remove the baking cups, turn the pupcakes upside down and add an extra piece of pineapple and a couple of blueberries for decoration

Yields about 10 pupcakes

# Fang Q Very Much

## "Oh, Mommy, a pussycat pupcake.
## Fang Q."

### *What you need:*

- 1½ cups whole wheat flour
- ¼ cup rolled oats
- 2 tsp bakng powder
- ½ tsp baking soda
- 1 tbsp dried mint (or 2 tbsp fresh chopped mint)
- ¼ cup vegetable oil
- 2 eggs
- 1 cup plain non-fat yogurt
- ½ cup 100% pure peanut butter
- 2 teaspoon rice syrup

### *What to do:*

- Preheat the oven to 350 F and prepare your muffin pans with baking cups
- Whisk the dry ingredients together in a large bowl

- Make a well in the center of the dry ingredients and drop in the eggs, oil, yogurt, peanut butter and rice syrup
- Whisk the wet ingredients together, gradually incorporating the dry mix.
- Stir in the mint
- Fill your baking cups with the batter
- Bake about 20 minutes for standard size pupcakes, 12 minutes for minis, or until a toothpick inserted in the middle of a pupcake comes out clean
- Cool for 2 or 3 minutes in the pan then remove to a cooling rack

*The pupcake pictured here was decorated following directions from the book, 'Hello, Cupcake!' You can recreate it using cream cheese frosting and black food dye, or use carob powder and make the cat brown.*
*For a more simple frosting, try the peanut butter recipe in Chapter 7.*

*Directions to create this Pupcake Dog are at the end of Chapter 7.*

# CHAPTER 7 – FROSTING

### For cream cheese frosting:

Bring the cream cheese to room temperature. Add a touch of rice syrup or low-fat plain yogurt then beat 'til light and easy to spread.

### For peanut butter frosting:

Use at room temperature. Drain off any oil on the top of the peanut butter, beat together with an equal amount of low-fat cream cheese. Spread lightly on the pupcakes.

### For variety:

- Color the cream cheese naturally with a little (*just* a little) carob or spirulina powder
- Add a small amount of pumpkin puree (not pie filling) to cream cheese
- Add a small amount of 100% pure applesauce to cream cheese
- Sprinkle peas or chopped/grated vegetables on cream cheese frosting, or cut vegetables into fun shapes
- Top cream cheese or peanut butter with fruit pieces
- Top with a mini dog biscuit or other treat

### Cottage cheese frosting:

A quick alternative to cream cheese frosting is to use cottage cheese. Just drain some of the moisture out of the cottage cheese by putting it in a sieve over a bowl, then beat 'til smooth. Stiffen with a little bone meal powder if needed.

*For Pupcake dog:*

- Add carob powder to cream cheese frosting.
- Create the body of the dog with a layer of frosted mini pupcakes then add a second layer on top, pressing the pupcakes firmly into place
- Use two pupcakes for each of the front legs, one each for the back legs and one for the tail
- Spread a layer of frosting over the front for the face
- Cut a pupcake in half and press it on to the face for the nose
- Fill a decorating bag with frosting and pipe strands over the whole dog to create a shaggy look, leaving the face untouched except for the nose (You may need to stiffen the frosting up by adding a small amount of flour. Go easy, though, you don't want to taste the flour)
- Pipe circles of plain cream cheese frosting for the eyes and add dog treats to the middle
- Chill, then mold frosting for the ears
- Candy has been used for the tongue and bow for decoration only. Remove these before giving to your pet.

## ABOUT THE AUTHOR

Muttster mixologist and culinary canine, Boo zeHound was trained at the CIA (Culinary Institute for Animals). Mr zeHound comes from a long line of canine gourmutts and first developed his nose for canine cuisine by sniffing out crumbs on the kitchen floor of his pet parents' home in Labrador, Alaska.

Growing up on the coast, Boo loved that his diet sometimes included wild salmon and cod. But it was hard to scratch a living in such a remote part of the world, so when Boo was just one year old the family moved to Dog Bluff, South Carolina, which unfortunately was almost as quiet as Labrador. So with nothing much to do but play dead dog, Boo decided it was time to go walkies on his own.

He worked his way through the garbage cans of some of the finest restaurants in the finest cities, took a licking from the best gourmutt chefs and barktenders in the country and eventually earned admission into the prestigious CIA, graduating later with the school's highest honors of five bones.

Mr zeHound is recognized as one of the pawmost experts in the field of doggy dishes and drinks and has joined forces with Elizabeth Dodwell to create this collection of healthy and delicious dogails and muttinis for discriminating dogs.

*Why not grab a copy of the companion book to our Pupcake recipes?*

# DOG TREATS: The BARKtender's Guide to Easy Homemade Dogtails and Muttinis

Printed in Great Britain
by Amazon